THE LIFE, WRITINGS
AND CHARACTER
OF
EDWARD ROBINSON

This is a volume in the Arno Press collection

AMERICA
AND
THE HOLY LAND

Advisory Editor
Professor Moshe Davis

Editorial Board
Professor Robert Theodore Handy
Professor Jules Davids
Dr. Nathan M. Kaganoff

See last pages of this volume for a complete list of titles.

THE

LIFE, WRITINGS AND CHARACTER

OF

EDWARD ROBINSON

Henry B[oynton] Smith
and
Roswell D. Hitchcock

ARNO PRESS

A New York Times Company

New York / 1977

Editorial Supervision: JOSEPH CELLINI

———◆———

Reprint Edition 1977 by Arno Press Inc.

AMERICA AND THE HOLY LAND
ISBN for complete set: 0-405-10220-8
See last pages of this volume for titles.

Manufactured in the United States of America

———◆———

Library of Congress Cataloging in Publication Data
Hitchcock, Roswell Dwight, 1817-1887.
    The life, writings, and character of Edward Robinson.

    (America and the Holy Land)
    Reprint of the 1863 ed. published by A. D. F.
Randolph, New York.
    1. Robinson, Edward, 1794-1863. 2. Congregationlists
--United States--Biography. I. Smith, Henry Boynton,
1815-1877, joint author. II. Title. III. Series.
BX7260.R62H5 1977   285'.8'0924   [B]   77-70744
ISBN 0-405-10299-9

77-9142

In tribute to
DANIEL G. ROSS
for his leadership, friendship and counsel

THE

LIFE, WRITINGS AND CHARACTER

OF

EDWARD ROBINSON, D.D., LL.D.,

READ BEFORE THE N. Y. HISTORICAL SOCIETY

BY

HENRY B. SMITH, D.D.,

AND

ROSWELL D. HITCHCOCK, D. D.

PUBLISHED BY REQUEST OF THE SOCIETY.

NEW YORK:

ANSON D. F. RANDOLPH,

683 BROADWAY.

1863.

EDWARD O JENKINS,
Printer,
20 North William Street.

REMARKS

OF

PROF. HENRY B. SMITH, D. D.,

ON THE ANNOUNCEMENT OF THE DEATH OF DR. ROBINSON,
AT A MEETING OF THE NEW YORK HISTORI-
CAL SOCIETY, FEBRUARY 3, 1863.

DR. EDWARD ROBINSON, though not able to trace his lineage to the spiritual father of the Plymouth Colony, was of Puritan descent and New England parentage. He was endowed in a high degree with the mental and moral qualities of that penetrating, frugal, laborious, liberty-loving and God-fearing race from which he sprung. His early advantages were slender, but they were all well improved. In Hamilton College he easily stood at the head of a large class in every department of study, though mathematics was at first his chosen pursuit. Devoting himself to the ministry of the Gospel, he soon found that his congenial sphere was in the walks of sacred scholarship rather than in the routine of pastoral life. At Andover and in Germany, during nine years of study, he prepared himself, with patient toil, for his life's work ; and with such sagacity and success, that the name of the humble New England boy is now named — in Sacred Geography, with those of Bochart, Reland and Ritter, in Sacred Philology, with Gesenius and Winer. In both these branches, as also in the editing of theological periodicals, and in the thorough training of a large number of students for the sacred ministry, his eminence is so undisputed, that no English scholar of the present century can be said to surpass him.

With a clear perception of the wants of the times, he first devoted himself to the thorough study of the original languages of the Bible. Forty-three years have elapsed since he first went to Andover and received a strong impulse from the ardent labors of Professor Stuart. Theological controversy in New England had already ceased to be chiefly metaphysical and dogmatic, and had begun to centre more definitely in the inquiry as to the exact sense of the Scriptural record. Sacred Philology was revived. Stuart was impulsive, and Robinson methodical; the one was bold, the other exact; the former inspired, the latter instructed with patient skill; what the one began with enthusiasm, the other perfected with elaborate care. Luther's motto, *Nulla dies sine linea*—the maxim of assiduous toil, and that other maxim of constant progress, *Dies diem docet,* which Gesenius put in the front of his Hebrew Lexicon, give us the clue to Dr. Robinson's scholarship. Such labor may be called plodding, but it is sure; thus alone can a thesaurus be made, a mine for all scholars. The process is slow, but the result is a monument, defying the tooth of time, and above the envy of the aspirants for fugitive applause. It is worthy of a noble ambition, and a high reward for years of toil, to be assured that a work has been completed to which scholars of every communion, in many lands, and through long years must resort, there to learn wisdom and knowledge.

I can only allude to what Dr. Robinson achieved for the grammar of the classic Greek and of the New Testament scriptures, by translations from the German; for Hebrew lexicography, by his edition of Gesenius; for sure and careful interpretation, by various essays and prolonged instruction; and above all, for the exegesis of the New Testament, by his unequaled Lexicon, itself a concordance of most of the words and a commentary on all the more difficult passages. His Harmony of the Gospels, too, has a high and deserved repute. But I may add a word on the principles which guided all his interpretations. His simple, single aim was to give the exact sense of the sacred writers, unprejudiced by dogmatic assumptions or preconceived theories. As the Germans say, he did not read *between* the lines, but he read the lines themselves. He belonged to the staid historico-philological school of exegetes —the school of Ernesti, Winer, Gesenius, De Wette, Tholuck, Meyer, and many other well-known philologians. He belonged to this school without sharing the rationalizing tendencies of some of its adherents, for he rested reverentially in the declarations of the Divine Word. He had no sympathy with either mysticism or rationalism. He accepted revealed mysteries without being a mystic, and he used all the lights of reason without being a rationalist. Disdaining the cheap notoriety which may be won by exaggerating difficulties, whether arithmetical, chronological, or geographical — he preferred the wisdom which attempts their explanation and harmony ; and where all was not yet clear, he struggled faithfully for further light. Because there are sometimes clouds in the sky, he did not deny the sun and the stars.

And so his criticism helped his faith, and also the faith of others. For those taught by him were forewarned, and not to be taken unawares by any new and adventurous display of old and oft-answered objections. And his confidence was ever firm, that the more God's word is studied, the more it will be prized. He feared not the progress of the sciences, nor any honest research ; believing that there is no disharmony between what Kepler calls " the finger and the tongue of God," his works and his word.

Geography, not less than philology, has grown in scientific dignity in these later days. The great Ritter has elevated it to a high position ; treating it not merely as a description of the material structure and outlines of the earth's surface, but also in its intimate and vital relations with the whole fauna and flora of creation, and especially as the abode of a rational race, the arena of human history. And among all the lands of the earth, the land of the Bible is still the one pervaded by the most hallowed memories, the theatre of the life of that wonderful people, which has given a faith to all civilized nations, and itself remains, dispersed all over the earth, bearing witness to the authenticity of its own records and confirming the prophecies of its own Books. The land of Abraham and of

Jacob, of David and Solomon, of the prophets of the old dispensation, and of the evangelists and apostles of the new—the land made holy by the presence of the Son of God—will always be sought out by the feet of pilgrims, and diligently investigated by the student of the Divine Word. This sacred region, sacked by the Romans and defiled by the Saracens, long remained in obscurity, but the irruptions of Crusaders in the middle ages made it again familiar to Europe ; and then many an ecclesiastic legend claimed to identify scenes and places named in the Word of God and the traditions of the Church. Exact investigations were needed even after the labors of Reland, Raumer, and Ritter. In two prolonged visits Dr. Robinson explored with a sharp eye and exact measurement all the most important sites ; and though he could not see much that others had reported, he certainly described many things which they had not observed ; though he dissipated some monastic fables and mediæval superstitions, he more than supplied

1.*

their place by accurate descriptions and certified results. He acted upon Cicero's rule, as applicable to geography as to history : *Prima historiæ lex est, ne quid falsi dicere audeat, ne quid veri non audeat.* He substituted scientific explorations for legendary lore ; and his four volumes on this subject have received from the best authorities the highest commendation. Unfortunately, the Manual, which was to digest all these researches, is not completed. But the results of his careful scrutiny are permanent. Here and there, a fact or statement may be revised by fresh explorations, but most even of the details are secure and trustworthy. Some of his positions have, indeed, been sharply impugned ; but Dr. Robinson, who never sought, did not avoid controversy ; and he was not a comfortable antagonist, because he judged by weight and measure. Hence he was seldom foiled. His works on the Holy Land stand at the head of the literature of this subject, not only in this country but in the civilized world.

What our revered colleague was as a professor and teacher, especially in the Union Theological Seminary for over twenty years, is known to more than a thousand pupils, chiefly ministers of the Gospel, now dispersed all over our own land, and in missionary stations afar off in the isles of the sea and to the ends of the earth— where his own missionary zeal so largely contributed in sending them. He could hardly visit a remote land in which his hand was not warmly grasped by a grateful scholar. Exact and punctual himself, he expected diligence and thoroughness in others. Every day he prepared himself anew for his task, because every day he was still a learner ; and, like all the great masters in science and art, he knew that progress is conditioned upon always having the elements of learning bright and burnished for daily use. His deep voice, sometimes strong and clear as a bell, gave weight and emphasis to his deliberate and clear conceptions. Now and then, having finished the details, or when challenged by a

special occasion, he would enter into the process
of a prolonged and luminous argument, no fact
neglected, no difficulty slurred over, which, in its
combined result, would produce a profound conviction and impression. And the honesty and
simplicity of his nature, his evident love of truth
for its own sake, always lent solidity and gravity
to his speech.

Francis Bacon—whom royal letters patent
needlessly and vainly authorize us to call Baron
of Verulam—tells us, that there are three kinds
of workmen : spiders, who spin all from their own
bowels ; ants, who simply collect ; bees, who
collect and work over.   Dr. Robinson is to be
ranked among the latter of these classes, having
left something, well worked over, for the benefit
of mankind.   He was emphatically a working
man, seduced neither by the pleasures of imagin-
ation, nor by the subtleties of metaphysical re-
finement.   A "large roundabout common sense"
characterized all he did and said.   An inflexible
honesty presided over his investigations.   Of

himself and his own works he rarely spoke, unless solicited, and then briefly ; but he was always ready to impart what he knew, that he might increase the sum of knowledge. Attached to the faith in which he was bred, he was never a polemic ; he never took part in ecclesiastical agitations ; he stood aloof from doctrinal controversy, and ever showed a truly catholic and magnanimous spirit. He chose his life's work, and did it well, faithful to the last.

In person, he was built upon a large and even massive scale ; with broad shoulders and muscular limbs, that denoted capacity for great endurance and toil ; crowned with a head of unusual volume, a broad and open forehead, with perceptive powers predominant ; a shaggy eye-brow, a full, bright, piercing eye, though usually shaded through infirmity ; a firm, yet pliant mouth ; and, altogether, giving the impression, even to a casual observer, of a man of weight and mark. His garments were worn for the sake of convenience and not of fashion.

His address was frank, direct, sometimes abrupt and decisive. Yet his affections were warm and deep ; he was tenacious in his friendships ; and the centre of his life was in his own home, adorned by the companionship of one, herself well known to fame. Any unusual expression of esteem or confidence would call forth a quick, responsive emotion. Intolerant of sentimentality, he honored all genuine feeling, and sympathized with whatever is noble and manly. An honest, earnest, resolute and self-reliant spirit, he also clung to others, and his soul was poised in God.

In his character, habits, association, and sympathies, he was every whit an American, and loved his country more, the more he knew of other lands. He died in the midst of the perils and darkness caused by the " weight of armies and the shock of steel ;" but he did not doubt the final triumph of the cause of liberty and law. His loyalty was heightened, when traitors struck down our flag ; his patriotism became more ardent when foreigners exulted in our anticipated ruin. Conservative by instinct, yet deeply sharing our national instinct— which is the love of an impartial liberty, he slowly but surely came to identify loyalty and liberty, and to see that our national cause is also freedom's cause.

Through almost all his mature life he was a sufferer from various bodily infirmities; yet with him, as with so many rare scholars, the disease of the mortal frame seemed but to stimulate the immortal energies of the soul, in its undying aspirations after knowledge and virtue. He labored often in pain, yet always in hope. Growing infirmities made him more genial, serene, and resigned; yet still he spoke little of himself. He lived in his work to the last. Though almost robbed of his mortal vision, he still spelled out to his classes the sacred words of the Book he prized above all others, and which gave to him an inner light. And within three months of three-score years and ten he had finished the work given him to do, and then he parted with that

> " earthly load of Death
> Called Life, which us from Life doth sever."

And upon his monument coming times will write

> Here lies an American Christian Scholar.

THE

LIFE, WRITINGS AND CHARACTER

OF

REV. EDWARD ROBINSON, D.D., LL.D.

READ BEFORE THE NEW YORK HISTORICAL SOCIETY,
MARCH 24, 1863.

BY

ROSWELL D. HITCHCOCK, D. D.

(17)

NOTE.

THE materials for the introductory part of the following discourse have been drawn from the Biography of the Rev. WILLIAM ROBINSON, written by his son, the Professor, and printed for private distribution in 1859. Should this part of the Discourse, at first sight, seem to be disproportionately long, the author hopes it will be found to have its use in throwing some light upon the character he has undertaken to portray.   R. D. H.

(18)

IN the Vatican there is a gallery, a thousand
feet in length, lined on either side with tablets, most of them sepulchral, taken from the
Catacombs of Rome. On the right are Pagan
tablets, chiseled with dreary, bitter, rebellious
sorrow. On the left are Christian tablets,
chiseled with tranquil resignation, trust, and
triumph. And so they stand confronting each
other: the Pagan and the Christian estimate
of death. On the one side is blind nature,
wringing her hands over an irreparable loss;
on the other, clear-eyed faith, bending meekly
over a form not dead, but only sleeping, whose
tenant has moved joyfully away, in full assur-
ance of a joyful return. On the one side there
is a passionate bewailing of hopelessly ruptured
ties; on the other, a serene recognition of un-
broken fellowship.

That gallery is now repeating itself in us. Here, as there, the Pagan antedates the Christian. Our first feeling is that of profoundest and most poignant grief. For ourselves, and for the scholarship of Christendom, we lament a soreness of bereavement seldom equaled. A great light, fed by the studies of half a century, has suddenly gone out, darkening our sky, darkening the whole firmament of letters. Nor had those studies fairly rounded their goal, as they might have done in two or three years more. The shaft that rose so steadily, has been denied its capital. The crowning work of that busy life, so long and eagerly revolved, so well outlined, and so well begun, has been left, and must remain, unfinished. The calamity is greater than of foundered ships, and lost battles.

And yet over against our great sorrow, there stands a greater consolation. This is no stroke of fate, but of Providence. To such as have lived aright it is gain to die. The service here, without arrest or interlude, joins on to a loftier service beyond the vail. Even as it regards ourselves, it may be that the departed, for all the finer uses of fellowship, are nearer to us than they were before. Or if there be no bond between us but that of memory, at all events, they rouse and rule us from their urns, as they never roused or ruled us with their living tongues. So death enriches while it robs us. It takes away our scholars, but turns them into sages. It takes away our Christian comrades, but turns them into saints. It thins our ranks upon the field, but quickens the conflict by new memories.

THE ANCESTORS OF DR. ROBINSON.

Dr. Edward Robinson, whose translation out of life into history we are now met to celebrate, was of the old Puritan stock of New England. The name naturally suggests descent from the famous John Robinson, first Pastor of the Plymouth Church, who led his little flock from Scrooby, in the north of England, to Amsterdam, and from Amsterdam to Leyden, where

he died in 1625, and whence his widow, and,
at least, one son, four years afterwards, mi-
grated to America. Such descent has, indeed,
been claimed in some branches of the family to
which our late associate belonged. But he himself, in a biography of his father, printed for
private distribution in 1859, sets aside this
claim, concluding his statement of the case with
the characteristic remark : " However much I
might rejoice in a rightful claim to an ancestry
so honorable, I am, nevertheless, loth to claim it
at the expense of historic truth." Quite recently, in 1855, it was discovered, that the Rev.
John Robinson, of Duxbury, through whom this
descent had been claimed, was of the Massachusetts Bay, and not of the Plymouth Colony. The
earliest ancestor of the family in this country
was William Robinson, of Dorchester. The
church in this town, whose organization in England preceded the settlement of the town itself
in 1630, was entirely broken up in 1635 by the
removal of the greater portion of its members,

with their minister, to Windsor, in Connecticut. In 1636 a new church was organized,
under the ministry of Rev. Richard Mather, the
father of Increase and grandfather of Cotton
Mather, then recently arrived from Bristol, in
England. Of this new church, William Robinson
became a member in 1636 or 1637. He was,
probably, from the west of England ; but no at-
tempt has been made, so far as I know, to carry
the genealogy any farther back. He was a
landed proprietor, the owner of a tide-mill still
extant in Dorchester, was once chosen Constable,
and three times Assessor, belonged to the "Ancient and Honorable" Artillery Company of
Boston, and in 1668 died a violent death, being
drawn through and torn to pieces by the cog-
wheel of his mill.

His eldest son, Samuel, acquired a still larger
property, and came to higher honor amongst his
fellow-townsmen ; receiving, as few then did, the
title of Mr., and holding at different times the
offices of Assessor, Selectman, and Representative

to the General Court. He died in 1718, at the
age of seventy-eight.

The third in descent was Rev. John Robinson, born in Dorchester in 1671, and graduated
at Harvard College in 1695 ; the scholarly but
eccentric minister of Duxbury, whose handsome
property, inherited from his father, enabled him
to collect a fine library, who went through the
coldest winters without a fire in his study,
preached always in a short jacket, eschewed
over-coats, had many sharp disputes with a
penurious people about his salary, finally resigned his pastoral charge, and, after a pretty
emphatic shaking off of the dust of his feet "as
an everlasting testimony" against the "vipers,"
removed to Lebanon, in Connecticut, the residence of his son-in-law, the first Governor Trumbull, where he spent the last six years of his life,
and died in 1745, at the age of seventy-four. His
wife was a descendant of John Alden, one of the
founders of the Plymouth Colony. The Plymouth separatism thus blended with the Massa-

chusetts Bay nonconformity in the views of the
Robinsons, as they had already blended in the
ecclesiastical life of New England.

The youngest son of this eccentric clergyman,
born in Duxbury in 1720, inherited at once the
Lebanon homestead, and his full share of the
paternal eccentricity. His name was Ichabod,
and he lived to be eighty-eight years old. By
appointment of his brother-in-law, Governor
Trumbull, then Probate Judge, he was for a
time Clerk of the Probate Court; but, with this
exception, rose to no higher civil trust than that
of Key-keeper and Guager. He was a man of
peevish temper and queer ways, jealous of his
relatives, the Trumbulls, the terror of all mis-
chievous urchins, not much loved even by his
own immediate family, and yet respected by his
neighbors, because really respectable by reason
of his intelligence and moral strictness. He
kept a store in Lebanon, buying his goods
chiefly in Boston, though sometimes importing
them from England; and made a comfortable

2

living by the business. Our Dr. Robinson remembered him, as he confesses, without affection,
and yet speaks with gratitude of the use he was
permitted to make of the old gentleman's library, which "contained many of the best works,
which appeared in England for the half century
prior to the American revolution." Special mention is made of the original edition of Defoe's
Robinson Crusoe, of the Spectator, and of the
Gentleman's Magazine, to which his grandfather
was for ten years a subscriber. We, in our turn,
must not fail to be grateful to this country mer-
chant, who permitted the hungry boy to "sit in
his great arm-chair, and devour his books." We
must also pass it to his credit, that, out of a slender income, he managed to bestow upon two
of his sons an education at Yale College.

THE FATHER OF DR. ROBINSON.

The second son of this Ichabod, was the Rev.
William Robinson, the father of our Professor.
His mother was Lydia Brown, a woman of strong

mind and energetic character, through whom he inherited, from the Browns, great size and strength of body, with great solidity of judgment. He was spared the inheritance of his father's and grandfather's eccentricities. He was his mother's boy, and his mother, who was always out of bed before daylight, used to take him with her. To this habit of early rising, thus formed, and adhered to through life, he ascribed no small share of his success. From the celebrated Grammar School of Master Tisdale in Lebanon, which, with the possible exception of that of Master Moody in Newburyport, was then the best school in New England, he went to Yale College, where he was graduated in 1773. Amongst his classmates were James Hillhouse, afterwards United States Senator ; Benjamin Tallmadge, Member of Congress ; and Nathan Hale, " the martyr-spy of the Revolution." One of his tutors in college was Joseph Lyman, afterwards the Rev. Dr. Lyman of Hatfield, Massachusetts ; between whom and himself there continued during their lives the most cordial friendship. As illustrating the commercial progress of the nation since then, it may be worthy of mention, that the average expenses of young Robinson in college, were only about seventy-five dollars a year. As indicative of his mental tone, it may also be mentioned, that, amongst the books purchased by him in his senior year, were Prideaux's Connection, Rollin's Ancient History, and Robertson's History of Charles the Fifth. Before graduating, he took the Blakeley prize for declamation, which that year was a copy of Mill's Septuagint ;* and when he graduated, it was with a high reputation both for ability and scholarship. After two years of teaching at Windsor, he returned to New Haven, and began to prepare for the Christian ministry, having Timothy Dwight and Joseph Buckminster, then tutors in the college, as his companions in

---

* It came into the possession of Dr. Robinson, and was used by him to the last. On the fly-leaf of the first volume is inscribed " Gulielmi Robinson's *Munus pro declamando,*" in the handwriting, probably, of President Daggett.

theological study. He commenced preaching in
1776 ; with what measure of success, may be in-
ferred from the effort made to induce him to
preach as a candidate in the pulpit once occupied
by Jonathan Edwards in Northampton. Declin-
ing this, and all other overtures, he continued to
reside in New Haven, one year as tutor in the
college, studying, and preaching as opportunities
offered, till 1780, when he settled down in
Southington, a town about half way between
New Haven and Hartford, where, after forty-one
years of service, he died on his birth-day, August 15th, 1825, just seventy-one years of age.
According to the estimate of his abilities entertained by those who knew him intimately, he
ought to have taken high rank amongst the theological giants of his day. In the type of his
theology, closely allied to Dr. Bellamy, it was
believed he might have rivaled him in influence.
Only two years younger than President Dwight,
he was, at the time, considered quite equal to him
" in intellectual power and promise." As com-

pared with Dr. Smalley, Dr. Chapin once ex-
pressed the opinion, that though Dr. Smalley
might be the more acute, Mr. Robinson had the
larger grasp and the wider vision, of the two. It
was evidently a matter of very painful reflection
to our friend the Professor, that his father did no
more to realize the expectations entertained of
him by his early contemporaries. The secret of
his comparative obscurity is easily discovered.
Commencing his professional life, when about
twenty-six years of age, in a farming town, at
that time one of the poorest in the State, with a
" settlement," as it was termed, of two hundred
pounds, and an annual stipend of barely one hundred pounds, with twenty-five cords of fire-wood,
the necessities of a growing family soon compelled him to cast about for other means of support. He became a farmer ; and, being a man
of shrewd, strong sense, he became an exceed-
ingly thrifty farmer. He bought fields and pas-
tures, cows and oxen, and also kept bees ; all of
which he used to let out on shares. He also

purchased a grist-mill, and a saw-mill. And with such rare sagacity and judgment did he manage all this business, as to make himself, in no long time, the wealthiest man in town. By and by, this secular enterprise and thrift began to be complained of. Not that the minister failed in the spiritual duties of his office ; for his mornings, and they had an early beginning, were always spent in his study, his preaching was instructive and solid, and pastoral visitation was by no means neglected. Not that he was charged with sharp, hard dealings, or inordinate gains ; for he greatly befriended the poor, was foremost in every public enterprise, and did more than any other man that ever lived in Southington towards developing its agricultural resources, and thus making the town what it now is. Not for any of these reasons was Mr. Robinson blamed, but simply because there was a good deal of human nature in Southington besides what was inside of the parsonage. Of the one hundred and seventy ministers at that time

in Connecticut, not one lived upon his salary, or
was expected to live upon it. They all half sup-
ported themselves. And some of them, whether
more fortunate, more frugal, or more sagacious
than others, acquired considerable estates. Even
Dr. Bellamy was very well off. The offence of
Mr. Robinson, as we are called upon to measure
it, was mainly against himself. His fault was,
that when he had secured a competency for himself and his family, he did not stay his hand, and
lay out his great strength in studies and efforts,
which might have won for him the leadership
for which nature designed him. If ever there
was real greatness undeveloped, which some
have questioned, here, doubtless, was an example of it in the person of the Rev. William Robinson of Southington. No one who reads the
memorial of him prepared by his distinguished
son, can fail to be struck by the many points of
resemblance between them. Unlike as they
were in their opportunities and achievements,
with respect to physical constitution, and certain

elements of character, one description might very
well answer for them both. The Connecticut
pastor was a man of large frame, and massive
head, with light sandy hair, and grey eyes over-
hung by shaggy brows. He had uncommon
depth and delicacy of sentiment, held in subjec-
tion by a clear understanding and a manly will.
Promptness, and severity of method, were conspicuous in all his doings. His opinions were
carefully matured, and then firmly adhered to.
Although, as his son says of him, " not a biblical
scholar after the present fashion," he had great
familiarity with the Scriptures, and laid special
stress upon Christian doctrine as the basis of
Christian life, and the inspiration of Christian
duty. In politics, he belonged to the school of
Washington, and could endure no man whose
principles appeared to him to be at war with
the virtue, the honor, or the institutions of his
country. As a preacher, he attempted no flights
of eloquence, but dealt out solid, sober truth, in
solid and sober style. His piety was a mascu-
2*

line conviction, mellowed by a tenderness too deep for voluble discourse. Dying of the same disease which took away his son, with few words, he gathered his mantle about him, and moved on calmly to meet his God.

Such, through all the generations of our American history, was the descent, and such the immediate parentage, of our great scholar. If we do not believe in hereditary rank, we must yet believe in blood. And of all human blood, none can be better than that of the old English Puritan, aërated for two such centuries on such a continent as this. New England may well be proud of having given such a scholar to the country. And the country may well be proud of having given such a scholar to the world.

His father was three times married, and three times a widower, within the first nine years of his residence in Southington. Of the four children by these earlier marriages, not one survives. His fourth wife was Elizabeth Norton of Farmington, a farmer's daughter; not elaborately edu-

cated, but of a good stock, the Rev. Dr. Asahel
Strong Norton, of Clinton, Oneida county, New
York, and Professor Seth Norton, of Hamilton
College, being her brothers; a woman of gentle
piety, of admirable sense, and always fond of
reading. She was the mother of six children
only three of whom are now living.* Her second son was our Edward, who was born in Southington, April 10th, 1794.

DR. ROBINSON'S EARLY LIFE.

Although the son of a clergyman, that clergyman, as we have seen, was also a farmer, carry-
ing on a large business; and it was this secular
side of the family life, which made itself most felt
in the early training of the son. His father's
library was not a large one. It contained the
writings of his distinguished contemporaries,
Bellamy, Hopkins, West, Smalley, Strong, and
Dwight; as also the works of the elder Edwards. These, with Ridgley's Body of Divinity,

* She died in 1824.

were about all that the library contained of systematic theology, till, in 1816, the Philadelphia edition of Calvin's Institutes was added. In the line of regular commentary, the only apparatus possessed was Poole's Annotations. The minister, it is true, spent the early hours of each day in his study ; and a chapter or two in the Greek Testament uniformly constituted a portion of his daily task. But the atmosphere of the house savored more of the farm than of the study. The common sitting-room of the family was the kitchen, whose most vividly remembered music in after years was "the busy hum of the spinning-wheels, both large and small," responded to by "the click of the loom in the wash-house." For many years, the clothing of the family, both linen and woolen, was all of home manufacture. The sons of the family, till the age of thirteen or fourteen, were brought up to labor with the hired men upon the farm. Edward, however, being of a slender constitution, shared only in the lightest of these labors. He was early noted

for his mechanical ingenuity. Many contriv-
ances, for the facilitating of manual labor in the
house and on the farm, attested at once his skill,
and his care for the comfort and happiness of the
family. He became an expert weaver ; a beautiful blanket of his handiwork being still carefully preserved as a memento of his youthful
industry. As described by one of his younger
brothers, Charles Robinson, Esq., of New Haven,
to whom I am indebted for these and other particulars of his early life, he was at this time remarkable chiefly for the kindliness of his disposition, the maturity of his practical judgment,
the soundness of his moral principles, and the
general propriety of his deportment. His brother
is of the opinion, that he had no great mental
precocity, and was not at first a remarkably
bright scholar ; but another member of the family has said, that his companions in the village
school always considered him the first scholar
among them. He was certainly very fond of
books, and if he lacked anything in quickness

and brilliancy, it was more than balanced by his eager thirst for knowledge, combined with an untiring industry and an iron diligence, which enabled him in the long run to outstrip all competition. He never missed an opportunity, and was never idle. " The loss of a minute," he once said to a younger brother who had laid down his book to eat an apple, " is just so much loss of life." And this was his watchword to the last.

Between the ages of ten and sixteen, having gone with credit through all the branches of study pursued in the common schools of his native town, he appears to have resided for some time as a pupil in the family of the Rev. Mr. Woodward of Wolcott, an adjacent parish. It is related of him as an eminently characteristic incident, that while residing in Wolcott, in the midst of a great excitement in regard to inoculation with kine pox as a protection against small pox, then a recent discovery, he took some of the virus home with him and successfully vaccinated the whole family. He was then about fifteen years of age, and had probably commenced his classical studies. Not far from the same time he taught school in Farmington, as also afterwards in East Haven ; in both of which places there are still a few surviving pupils, who remember him and his instructions with lively interest and affection.

As his father, for some reason or other, had no idea of sending him to college, and his constitution was not rugged enough for the life of a farmer, he was put, when sixteen years of age, as an apprentice into the store of a Mr. Whittlesey, of Southington. Here he had special charge of the drugs, which made up a part of the stock in trade. But his desire for knowledge, which had by this time become a passion, rebelled against the arrangement, so that, after a couple of years, he was prepared and permitted to join his maternal uncle, Professor Seth Norton, at Clinton, New York, where he entered the first Freshman class of Hamilton College, in the autumn of 1812.

HIS CONNECTION WITH HAMILTON COLLEGE.

His scholastic career was now fairly begun. His uncle, Professor Norton, then thirty-two years of age, was a good classical scholar, and a very successful teacher. His tutor in mathematics was Theodore Strong, since then a distinguished professor and author. Some three or four years ago Dr. Robinson was heard to say, that of all his teachers Mr. Strong was the one who had done most towards shaping his course in life by thoroughly rousing his mind to study. The college, it is true, was just commencing its existence on the very verge of the wilderness, and almost within sight of the wigwams of the Oneidas. But the class to which young Robinson belonged, considering the infancy of the institution, was quite respectable in numbers, and more than respectable in ability and promise. Of the seventeen whose names are now in the Triennial catalogue, two have been members of Congress, two have received

the title of D. D., and three the title of LL. D.
Of the six or more who have died, one was the
Rev. Luther F. Dimmick, D. D., a highly respected and influential clergyman of Newburyport, Massachusetts. Of those who survive, the
Hon. Philo Gridley of Utica, Judge of the Supreme Court of New York, and the Hon.
Charles P. Kirkland of New York city, are too
well known to require remark. Robinson was
the eldest of them all, being at the time he
entered college eighteen years of age. Of his
personal character and habits as a student, not
much was then known, or if known, not now
remembered, by his surviving associates. He
lived very much by himself; moved thereto, not
more by the disparity of age between himself
and his classmates, than by his greater maturity
of character and aim. His rank as a scholar
was soon determined. In every branch of study,
and equally in all, he stood easily, and without a
rival, at the head of his class. He was then
especially fond of mathematics, for which his

natural aptitude, perhaps, was greatest, but was also an accurate linguist, and was crowned with acclamation by his classmates as the finest writer of them all. So strongly pronounced was his ability, and so remarkable his diligence, that those who knew him then, would have been greatly disappointed, had he failed of a distinguished career.

To what employment he first betook himself after his graduation in 1816, I have not been able to learn. But in February, 1817, he repaired to Hudson, New York, where he spent the summer in the law office of James Strong, Esq., afterwards member of Congress. Had he pushed on in this direction, we should now, perhaps, be lamenting the decease of one of the ablest jurists in the land. A very different destiny awaited him, towards which he was now beckoned by the offer of a tutorship in Hamilton College. Accepting this appointment, he returned to Clinton, and for one year gave instruction in mathematics and Greek. This service ended, in the early autumn of 1818 [September 3d], he was married to Eliza Kirkland, youngest daughter of the Rev. Samuel Kirkland, the well-known Missionary to the Oneidas, a man of strong character, and almost romantic life. To benefit the Indians, amongst whom he had labored, he founded the Oneida Academy at Clinton, out of which grew Hamilton College, as Dartmouth College had previously grown out of Dr. Wheelock's Indian school, first established at Lebanon, Connecticut, and afterwards removed to Hanover, New Hampshire. One of his three sons was the brilliant John Thornton Kirkland, President of Harvard College,* and author of the biography of Fisher Ames, one of the choicest of our American classics. One of his three daughters was the mother of the Rev. Dr. Lothrop of Boston. The youngest was Eliza, some years older than Mr. Robinson, but a woman of superior intellect and edu-

* From 1810 to 1828. He died in 1840, at the age of seventy.

cation, and of uncommon personal attractiveness.
She died in less than a year after their mar-
riage, leaving him in possession of the large and
fine farm inherited from her father, who had
died some years before.* Here Mr. Robinson
continued to reside, dividing his time between
study and the care of the farm, till the autumn
of 1821, when he went to Andover, Massachusetts, for the purpose of publishing his first
book. This was an edition of eleven books of
the Iliad—the first nine, the eighteenth and the
twenty-second, with a Latin introduction, notes,
and other apparatus of study ; a reproduction,
for the most part, of the editorial labors of
Heyne, Wolf, and others, but with some changes,
and many omissions and additions. This volume
probably affords us an indication, not only of
what his recent studies had been, but also of his
literary plans and aspirations for the future.
He appears to have chosen the Greek language
and literature as his study for life.

* In 1808.

AT ANDOVER.

But at Andover he fell under the singularly magnetic influence of Professor Moses Stuart, who soon launched him in a new direction. His Iliad was put to press in May, 1822. About this time he is remembered, by one who was then a member of the Junior class in the Theological Seminary,* as discussing, in the tone of a novice, the Hebrew vowel points, which Professor Stuart had but recently been willing to adopt. But when once fairly started, so rapid was his progress, that in the autumn of 1823, Professor Stuart had him appointed Instructor in Hebrew in the Seminary. Upon him in a great measure devolved the labor of correcting the proof sheets of the second edition of Stuart's Hebrew Grammar, which appeared in September, 1823. In the preface, credit is given him " for many of the improvements in manner, not a few in matter, and

* The Rev. O. Eastman, one of the secretaries of the American Tract Society, who then occupied a room, as did also Mr. Robinson, in the house of the Rev. Dr. Woods.

for much of the minute accuracy" of the new edition. Professor Stuart then goes on to say, that " the radical knowledge which Mr. Robinson has acquired of this language, is a happy indication of the progress which the study of it is making in our country ; and holds out in regard to him a promise of extensive usefulness in the department of sacred literature." So much had he accomplished in less than two years. " Whether scribe or pharisee," as he said of himself playfully, and not without some just pride, " he had been put into Moses' seat." Admirably did he sustain himself in this difficult position for three years, from 1823 to 1826. Right under the eye, and under the dazzling reputation of the Magnus Apollo of biblical scholarship in America, he held his place with marked ability, and succeeded in making a reputation of his own. If Stuart was the more brilliant, adventurous, and electric, firing his pupils with enthusiasm, Robinson was looked upon as the more careful, exact, and thorough. He

was a most indefatigable student. There seemed
to be no end to his endurance of mental toil. As
a teacher, he was dry, but clear and strong. His
patient and solid scholarship commanded the un-
qualified respect of all competent judges, and
made him a conspicuous candidate for future fame
as an Orientalist. His leaning, however, was
decidedly towards the Greek, rather than the Hebrew language. This appears in his translation
of Wahl's *Clavis Philologica Novi Testamenti*,
with some additions and improvements, which he
published at Andover in 1825; as also in the association of his name with that of Professor Stuart,
in a translation of the first edition of Winer's
Grammar of the New Testament Greek, which
was put forth in the same year. Winer's Grammar, it is true, was "a mere pamphlet," and
Wahl's *Clavis* was soon outgrown by the scholarship which had reproduced it on this side of
the Atlantic; but these translations marked the
beginning amongst us of a new era in the domain
of biblical criticism. They were the early

sheaves of a rich harvest, which has been equaled nowhere outside of Germany.

RESIDENCE IN GERMANY.

In 1826, having resigned his place at Andover,
Mr. Robinson, who was then thirty-two years of
age, set sail for Europe, in quest of philological
opportunities and helps, such as Europe only
could afford. After staying awhile in Paris,
where the venerable De Sacy was still vigorously
at work,* he made his way to Germany, first
spending a few weeks at Göttingen, to get well
started in the language, and then going to Halle
where he plunged into his favorite studies, with
so clear a vision of what he wanted, and so determined a purpose in its pursuit, as could not fail to
to insure an accomplished scholarship. In steady,
plodding diligence, he became a German amongst
the Germans. He remained four years abroad,
residing mostly at Halle and Berlin, but making
himself familiar with other interesting localities

* He died in 1838.

in Germany, and visiting the northern countries
of Europe, as well as France, Switzerland, and
Italy. His residence in Germany was well-timed.
Many eminent scholars, since deceased, were
then in their prime. At Halle were Gesenius,
Wegscheider, and Thilo, who have since died;
besides Tholuck and Rödiger, who are still alive.
At Berlin were Buttmann, Hegel, Schleiermacher,
Marheineke, Neander, Zumpt, Ritter, and Savig-
ny, all now gone; with Hengstenberg, Bekker,
and Bopp, who are still among the living. At
Göttingen he found the two Plancks, father and
son, Pott, Blumenbach, Heeren, and Lücke, not
one of whom survives. Those with whom he appears to have had most to do, were Gesenius,
Tholuck and Rödiger at Halle, and Neander at
Berlin. Gesenius, in 1826, was about forty years
of age, and was at the height of his reputation,
with five hundred students crowding his lecture
room. Tholuck was but twenty-seven years of
age, and had only just come to Halle. Rödiger,
the exact grammarian, a favorite pupil of Gese-

3

nius, and now, perhaps, the finest Arabic scholar
living, was younger still, and did not begin to
teach at Halle till 1828. Neander, at the time
Mr. Robinson was in Berlin, was thirty-eight
years old, and had issued the first volume of his
History two years before. Our American scholar
did not put himself in contact with any of these
men, to be moulded by them. He had by nature
too much intellectual independence, and was by
discipline too mature a thinker, to be bent away
from the line of development, in which, on the
other side of the Atlantic, and under the influence of other institutions, he had begun to move.
And yet he learned much of his German teachers
and companions in study. Gesenius he admired
as " the first Hebrew scholar of the age." Neander he regarded as not only " the first ecclesiastical historian of the age," but also as " one of
the best, if not quite the best exegetical lecturer
on the New Testament in Germany." Towards
Tholuck he was drawn not merely by " his uncommon and unquestioned talents and learning,"

but also by the fervency of his religious life. But whatever may have been his indebtedness to living teachers and scholars, the great advantage he reaped from his residence in Germany, was the perfect mastery it gave him of the German language, and thus of all the treasures of criticism which that language contains. But Germany's best gift to him was that of a domestic companion, who, for his sake, consented to surrender associations and plans and prospects, such as have rarely been surrendered by any woman for any man. Therese Albertine Luise von Jacob was the youngest daughter of Staatsrath von Jacob,* Professor of Philosophy and Political Science in the University of Halle. She was born and had lived in Halle till the family were driven out by the storm of war which burst upon that part of Germany in 1806. After ten years of exile in Russia, first at the University of Charkow and then at St. Petersburg, Professor von Jacob returned with his family to Halle. Mr.

* Who died in 1827.

Robinson was introduced to their social evening reunions by one of their relatives, who chanced to travel with him from Göttingen to Halle, as an American gentleman who "spoke but little German, and was melancholy and rather homesick." His natural reserve and bashfulness, aggravated by his imperfect knowledge of the language, were at first very much against him. But all this was presently overcome. There was one at least who recognized in him a man of no ordinary powers. And she herself, introduced to public notice by Goethe, had already attained distinction as a writer. They were married on the 7th of August, 1828. After spending nearly a year in Switzerland, France, and Italy, they returned to Halle, where they remained through the winter of 1829–30, Mr. Robinson abandoning with extreme reluctance the plan he had formed of wintering in England. On the 2d of July, after a tedious voyage of two months, they landed in America. Of the years that have followed, years of sacred domestic tenderness, not less than of diversified literary toil, and splendid literary achievement, I may not presume to speak. It is not for me to unveil either those ministries of love which once gladdened, or these vigils of heavy sorrow which are now hallowing the scholar's home.

PROFESSORSHIP AT ANDOVER.

Shortly after his return from abroad in 1830, Mr. Robinson was appointed Professor Extraordinary of Sacred Literature and Librarian at Andover. He had now reached the fulness of his strength, and began at once to put it forth in a succession of labors, as remarkable for their variety as for their value. In January, 1831, appeared the first number of the "Biblical Repository," of which he was the founder and sole editor, and which, for four years, was conducted by him with an ability and judgment that gave it almost oracular authority on both sides of the Atlantic. He himself furnished a large proportion of the matter which filled its pages. Of the one hundred and one articles contained in the first four volumes, forty-seven were from his own pen ; twenty of which were original essays, and twenty-seven translations and compilations, the translations being chiefly from the German. Two learned articles on " the Slavic language in its various dialects," were from the pen of Mrs. Robinson. Fourteen original essays were furnished by his colleague, Professor Stuart. The other thirty-eight articles were contributed by several scholars, most of whom are well known, and of acknowledged authority, in the theological world. " The Review," which was finally (in 1851) united with the " Bibliotheca Sacra," continued for some years longer to maintain a high rank ; but the earlier volumes, edited by Professor Robinson, are more sought after than all the rest. Beyond most other works of the kind, they are laden with matter of permanent value, and are of special interest as representing the first grand impulse given to the evangelical theology of America by the evangelical theology of Germany. The Doctorate of Divinity conferred upon Professor Robinson by Dartmouth College, in 1831, came none too early; he had earned it by contributions to sacred literature, not only valuable in themselves, but full of promise for the future.

His retirement from the editorship of the Biblical Repository by no means terminated his connection with the periodical press. He continued to furnish articles of value from time to time for the Repository; and, in 1843, commenced in New York a serial issue of tracts and essays on biblical and theological topics, many of them written by himself, which he called the *Bibliotheca Sacra*. In 1844, this work was transferred to Andover, and became a quarterly, under the editorial management of Professors Edwards and Park. For this also he continued to write as late as 1855, and allowed his name to remain upon the title-page till 1857. Of the articles furnished, many of which were geographical, special mention should be made of a suggestive and stimulating essay on " The Aspect of Literature and Science in the United States as compared with Europe ;" besides articles on " The Resurrection and Ascension of our Lord," " The Nature of our Lord's Resurrection-Body," and " The alleged Discrepancy between John and the other Evangelists respecting our Lord's Last Passover," which are models of thoroughness, and very valuable contributions to the exegetical literature of our language.

In 1832, Dr. Robinson edited Taylor's translation of Calmet's Dictionary of the Bible, greatly enhancing the value of it by such retrenchments and additions as his more critical and extensive scholarship enabled him to make. This portly work, of more than a thousand pages, went rapidly through a large number of editions ; but as he had no copyright in it, and was soon immersed in other studies, he bestowed no further labor upon it, and gave no further attention to it, except to make it the basis of a much smaller work, which, under the title of "A Dictionary of the Holy Bible, for the use of Schools and Young Persons," was issued by Crocker & Brewster, of Boston, in 1833. This same year, Buttmann's Greek Grammar was given to the American public, in a translation which he had made of it during the last winter of his residence in Halle. With such favor was this work received, and so steady continued the demand for it, that, in 1839, while Dr. Robinson was in Germany, on his way home from Palestine, his friend, Professor Stuart, was constrained to put forth, though without change, a second edition of it. This edition also soon went out of print. Another edition was long and loudly called for. Meanwhile, five new editions of the original, by Buttmann's son, had been published in Germany ; in the last two of which, there had been an almost entire reconstruction of the syntax, with improvements and additions throughout the whole work. In 1850, Dr. Robinson took in hand the eighteenth German edition of this

3*

bulky grammar, as, more than twenty years before, he had taken in hand the thirteenth, and
so made Buttmann once more a teacher in our
schools.

Dr. Robinson spent three years at Andover.
He was there as Professor Extraordinary, no
endowment existing for his support. Professor
Stuart had encouraged him to expect that such
an endowment would be secured; but, unfortunately for the Seminary, it did not come.
Meanwhile Dr. Robinson was taxing the strength
of his constitution beyond all prudent bounds.
Repeated attacks of epilepsy threatened his life.
It is true he got the better of this malady, but
his constitution was for the time shaken, and his
health was utterly broken down.* He therefore resigned his office, and in 1833 removed to
Boston.

* For a medical statement of the case, see Dr. Mussey's
recent book, "Health: its Friends and its Foes." Boston,
1862. Pp. 289–96.

IN BOSTON.

In Boston, as soon as his health permitted, he resumed his studies with renewed ardor, subject to none of the interruptions incident to the calling of a theological professor. The first fruit of these studies was, in 1834, a revised edition of Newcome's Greek Harmony of the Gospels, on the basis of Knapp's text. It was a great improvement upon the Andover edition of 1814; and a still greater improvement upon the original Dublin edition of 1778. And yet no radical changes were made. The work was still essentially Newcome's; his chronological order being generally followed, and his preface, sectional divisions and notes retained. Eleven years later, in 1845, Dr. Robinson published a Greek Harmony of his own, which was wholly a new and independent work. Its leading features were, the substitution of Hahn's text for that of Knapp; a new chronological arrangement in several important particulars, but especially of the events belonging to the last six months of our Lord's life; and the appended notes, substituted for those of Newcome, remarkable for the exactness and solidity of their learning. The more important changes referred to, grew out of his own identification, in 1838, of the city of Ephraim mentioned in John xi. 54, with the modern Taiyibeh, some twenty miles north of Jerusalem.* This established a parallelism between John xi. 54 and Luke xiii. 22, and enabled him to harmonize those portions of Matthew, Mark and Luke, which had previously been the most difficult to dispose of. This Greek Harmony immediately took its place at the head of all similar works. The London Religious Tract Society soon issued an English Harmony, based upon and almost entirely following Dr. Robinson's arrangement.† It was

---

* See *Bibliotheca Sacra*, vol. ii. pp. 398–400.

† Only a few and slight changes were made, on the authority of Greswell's *Harmonia Evangelica*, 1830–34, and Wieseler's *Chronologische Synopse*, 1843.

also taken as the basis of a French Harmony,
which was published in Brussels in 1851. In
1846, Dr. Robinson himself put forth an English
Harmony, making such changes in the notes as
seemed advisable in order to adapt them to
popular use, but making no change in the order
of time, except to correct a slight error of *one
day* in the Greek Harmony, into which he had
been led, as he says, " by relying too implicitly
upon the authority of the learned Lightfoot."
A revised edition of the Greek Harmony was
published in 1851.

But in Boston, during the three years which
he spent there, his strength was laid out mainly
in the department of Biblical Lexicography.
The 1815 edition of the Hebrew-German Lexicon of Gesenius, had been translated by Professor Gibbs in 1824 ; and this was followed by
an abridged Manual in 1828, which passed into
a second edition in 1832. But, during all this
time, Gesenius himself had been making rapid
progress in his favorite science ; so that his

Hebrew-Latin Lexicon, which appeared in 1833, was greatly in advance of all he had done before. This new work, the best Lexicon of any language which the world had seen, being the first to exemplify the historico-logical method of lexicography, was faithfully translated by Dr. Robinson, and laid before the public in 1836. A second edition, with additional matter from the *Thesaurus* of Gesenius, was published in 1842. A third edition, a good part of which was stereotyped, with further additions from the *Thesaurus*, appeared in 1849 ; a fourth edition in 1850 ; a fifth, and the last in which any changes were made, in 1854. Dr. Robinson was careful to say, that he performed no other office in connection with this work than that of a translator, adding nothing of his own, except an occasional remark or reference, always with his signature. The changes which Gesenius himself made in his own work, Dr. Robinson was but too happy to incorporate into the successive issues of the translation, since Gesenius so frankly confessed, that, "the older he grew, the more inclined he was to return in very many cases to the long received method of interpretation."

But the labor bestowed upon his first edition of Gesenius, occupied only a small portion of each day. Throughout the whole of the three years, during which this work was in hand, the greatest portion of every day was spent upon another work, which is now one of the main pillars of his fame. I allude to his *Greek and English Lexicon of the New Testament*. This also came from the press in the autumn of 1836, and was generally recognized at once as the best Lexicon of the New Testament in any language. The way had been well prepared for this new work. In his translation of Wahl's *Clavis*, years before, Dr. Robinson had, in two important respects, improved upon the original. The various constructions of verbs and adjectives with their cases, given only in part by Wahl, were given by Dr. Robinson in every instance. He also greatly multiplied the Scripture

references, so that the Lexicon became, in more
than seven-eighths of the words, a complete
Concordance of the New Testament. In some
points of interpretation he had found occasion
to differ with Wahl. One article, πνεῦμα, an
article of no little importance, he had entirely
recast. In short, he had gone so far in the matter of making changes, that it seemed to be both
his right and his duty to drop Wahl altogether,
and prepare a Lexicon of his own. This he now
did. The *Clavis*, a new edition of which had
appeared in 1829,* was, evidently, the founda-
tion upon which he built ; and properly enough,
since it was the best existing Lexicon of the New
Testament, and much of what enters into every
good Lexicon must needs be common property.
Bretschneider's *Manual*, which had reached a
second edition in 1829, was also freely used.†
Schleusner, likewise, was of some service to

* Wahl died in 1855. There have been three editions of
his *Clavis :* in 1822, 1829 and 1843.
† Bretschneider's *Manual* has appeared in three editions:
1824, 1829, and 1840.

him.* But Schleusner, in some important respects, was far behind the times in his scholarship ; and even with Wahl and Bretschneider he had points of difference on every page. Dr. Robinson's Lexicon was, therefore, in every just sense of these terms as employed in such a connection, a new and independent work. As such it was received, and received with great avidity; three rival editions of it being speedily issued in Great Britain. And yet when he sat down in 1847 to revise it for a new edition, so far was it from answering his own demands, that he re-wrote a large part of it. This great labor, which must have taxed his patience to the utmost, consumed three full years. These three years added to the three he had spent upon the first edition, and these again to the two years, which he had probably bestowed upon the *Clavis* of Wahl, make in all eight years of severe toil, the fruit of which is given us in the Lexicon of

* Schleusner died in 1831. His Lexicon was published in 1792, 1800, 1808, and 1819.

1850. It is, unquestionably, the best Lexicon
of the New Testament in existence. The method
of Gesenius is rigidly applied throughout, so far
as that method can be applied to the New Testament lexicography. The meanings of words
are traced, from the root, in their true logical
order. The discriminations are sharp. The
references to the Septuagint, to the later and to
the Attic Greek, are abundant and apposite.
In nine-tenths of the words, instead of the seven-
eights of the previous edition, the Lexicon is a
complete Concordance of the New Testament;
so that the student may almost dispense with
Bruder. And, furthermore, so much care has
been taken to interpret all the more difficult
passages, that the Lexicon is not only a Concordance, but also a Commentary. One may not
always agree with the Commentator, but if he
finds peace in his disagreement, he will have to
wrestle for it. A singularly self-possessed and
vigorous intellect challenges his judgment at
every step.

REMOVES TO NEW YORK.

In 1837, soon after publishing the first edition of his Lexicon, Dr. Robinson came to New York. He had been solicited, the year before, to accept a chair in the University of New York, but declined it. The Union Theological Seminary, then recently established, was more successful in its suit. He signified his willingness to accept the offered Professorship of Biblical Literature, on the condition of being permitted, before entering upon its duties, to be absent for three or four years for the purpose of exploring the Holy Land. This condition acceded to, he set sail, with his family, from New York, July 17, 1837; passed rapidly through England to the continent; up "the glorious Rhine" to Frankfort; and from Frankfort to Berlin, when he bade adieu to his family, and set his face towards the Orient. In Athens, he trod the Acropolis with all the enthusiasm of a scholar; but not till he had first set his foot upon the Areopagus with all the reverence of a Christian. In Egypt, he saw the Pyramids, and ascended the Nile to Thebes. From Egypt, along the route taken by the Hebrews, he went to Sinai; and from Sinai, by way of Akabah, to Palestine. His travelling companion was the Rev. Eli Smith, since deceased, missionary of the American Board, an accomplished Arabic scholar; and, between them, they searched the Land of Promise to somewhat better purpose than Caleb and Joshua. They started from Cairo March 12th. 1838; were at Sinai on the 23d; reached Jerusalem April 14th; explored Arabia Petræa in May; were at Nazareth June 17th; went from Nazareth to the Lake of Tiberias; from there to Safed; and from Safed, by way of Tyre and Sidon, to Beirut, where their journey ended June 27th. Hastening back to Germany, by way of the Danube, Dr. Robinson fell sick in Vienna, and barely escaped with his life. This severe sickness at Vienna was a crisis in his life. From this time, the exclusively vegetable diet prescribed for him some years before at Andover, was abandoned, and his health underwent a marked improvement. In October he got to Berlin ; and in August, 1840, after nearly two years of severe but delightful labor amidst the libraries and scholars of the most learned capital in Europe, the manuscript of his *Biblical Researches* was ready for the press.

These two years in Berlin were among the happiest and most golden of his life. He saw much of Neander, Hengstenberg, Twesten, Bopp, Zumpt, Raumer, Ranke, and Petermann, although the work upon which he was engaged left him but little time for society. With Karl Ritter, the great geographer, whose personal acquaintance he then made, he was especially intimate. Ritter was a man after his own heart ; learned, modest, generous, and of most unaffected and fervent piety. Common tastes and studies drew them very closely together. In 1852, when Dr. Robinson was again in Berlin, on the eve of his departure, Ritter gave him a flattering proof of his affection. As he came to take tea with him for the last time, he said : " I came near losing this evening. The King sent for me, but I sent word to his Majesty, that I must be excused this time, as it was the last evening which I could spend with my friend Robinson." And it was indeed the last, for Ritter died in 1859, and Dr. Robinson was not again in Germany till 1862.

The original manuscript of the *Researches* is now in the Library of the Union Seminary, neatly bound up in eighteen volumes; a precious treasure to us, as it will be more and more precious to those who come after us. In Berlin, it was translated into German by a competent hand, carefully revised by Mrs. Robinson, and afterwards carried through the press at Halle by Professor Rödiger. The sheets struck off in Boston were sent, in advance of their publication here, to London ; so that in 1841 the work was issued simultaneously in America, in England, and in Germany. The publication of this work was followed, in 1842, by what he looked upon as the highest of all his earthly honors : the awarding to him of a gold medal by the Royal Geographical Society of London. This gave him a place among the selectest few of scientific discoverers. Other academic honors which followed close, were, in 1842, the degree of D. D. from the University of Halle, and in 1844, the degree of LL. D. from Yale College.

In the autumn of 1851, the Directors of the Union Seminary, without solicitation on his part, though well aware of his desire in the matter, voted him leave of absence for another tour in Palestine. He left New York in December; spent a month in Berlin with Ritter, Lepsius, Humboldt, and other eminent men of science; sailed from Trieste by way of Smyrna to Beirut, where he landed April 5th, 1852 ; went through Galilee and Samaria once more, but by a new route, to Jerusalem ; carefully explored the more northern portions of the country, which he had failed to see on his former visit ; passed over to

Damascus; went up through Coele-Syria to Baalbek and Ribleh; crossed the mountains to El Husn; and from El Husn passed down southward to Beirut, where he arrived June 19th; on the 17th of July, joined his family at Salsburg, amongst the Austrian Alps; and on the 27th of October, was back again in his chair at the Seminary. On this second journey, he had as companions in successive stages of his route, the Rev. Eli Smith, as before; the Rev. W. M. Thomson; and the Rev. S. Robson; to all of whom he renders due tribute of acknowledgment for important services rendered him. In 1856, he gave us the new volume of his *Researches;* Mrs. Robinson, as he went on with the preparation of it, translating it for him into German.

He looked upon this as the great work of his life; and yet not this, but another, of which I shall presently speak, and of which this was to be but the preparation and the prelude. As far back as the time of his first residence in Germany, inspired by his love for the Word of God, he had conceived the design of exploring the Land of God. Through many laborious years, his studies were shaped with reference to it ; so that when the auspicious hour came for him to start, he was well prepared to make the most cf his opportunities. Men of learning, like Bochart and Reland, had treated of the Geography of Palestine, without having personally explored it ; Reland, most admirably, Bochart not.* On the other hand, unlearned men in abundance had traversed Palestine, and returned to repeat and perpetuate its monkish legends. Only Raumer, Burckhardt, and Laborde had written books of any great value to science. Even the map of Syria by *Berghaus*, till then the best, was found to be so inaccurate as to be of little service. The time had come for a scholar, equal to Reland in acuteness and breadth of judgment, to enter this tempting field with thermometer,

* The *Hierozoicon* of Bochart is of permanent value; but his *Geographia Sacra* abounds with "untenable hypotheses and and strained etymologies."

4

telescope, compass, and measuring-tape, but, above all, sharp-eyed and sufficiently skeptical, and then make report of what he had seen and measured. Such a man was our late associate, raised up, endowed, and trained, for this very purpose ; so keen of vision, that nothing escaped his notice ; so sound and solid of judgment, that no mere fancy could sway him ; so learned, that nothing of any moment pertaining to his work, was unknown to him ; and yet, withal, so ardent in his religious affections, as to pursue his task like a new Crusader. There never was a man better suited to his calling.

Of this great work, the *Biblical Researches,* in which his achievements of discovery are now enshrined, we have no need to speak. Since Ritter has pronounced its encomium, its authority is sealed, and its fame is fixed. In form, this work is a journal, after the manner of Maundrel and Burckhardt. On this are engrafted, at great cost of time and toil, historical illustrations and discussions " of various points relating

to the historical topography of the Holy Land."
The materials out of which the work was
wrought, were the very full separate journals
kept by Dr. Robinson and his travelling companion, which were usually written up each
night from pencil notes taken upon the spots
visited during the day. Dr. Robinson was of
the Poet Gray's opinion, that "a single line
written upon the spot, is worth a whole cart-
load of recollection." Of his indebtedness to
Dr. Eli Smith, which has been sometimes not
very generously alluded to, Dr. Robinson makes
repeated and most frank acknowledgment. The
more important and interesting results of the
journey, he says, are mainly to be ascribed to
the Arabic scholarship, and other accomplish-
ments, of his travelling companion.

HIS UNFINISHED WORK.

And yet this great work, which will send his
name down through every human generation to
the end of time, was but preparatory to another,

to which, through long years and consuming
studies, he looked steadily forward as the crowning labor of his life. In 1856 he wrote as fol-
lows : " The great object of all these travels and
labors has been, as formerly announced, to collect materials ' for the preparation of a systematic work on the physical and historical geography of the Holy Land.' To this work, so
much needed, should my life and health be
spared, I hope speedily to address myself." To
this work he did address himself, and that immediately. Even before the last sheets of his
later Researches had left his hands, he had set
about the new and final task. But instead of
any report of my own, I prefer to transcribe the
account kindly furnished me by Mrs. Robinson :

"In the year 1855 or 1856, while his later
Researches were printing, he commenced a work
on the Geography of the Bible, which he called :
"*Scripture Geography.*" Of this work, which he
divided into five parts, I find the full plan, the

introduction, and seventy closely written quarto pages ; besides notes, additions, etc.

"In this work he was interrupted by an attack of gastric fever during the winter of 1856–7. He never considered himself as perfectly cured during the following summer ; and this opinion was confirmed by another severe attack in 1857–8 of the same complaint, assuming a typhoid character, which greatly prostrated him. Although he felt decidedly better of that, it was some time before he could make up his mind to resume his more severe studies. He wrote the memoir of his father meanwhile. Of course, he kept thinking of his great work, and examining it from all sides ; but when he took it up again he decided to recast it completely, and began on the 3d of June, 1859, to write a new work. I find the full title of it written out by him : *Biblical Geography.* Vol. I. The Central Region : Palestine, with Lebanon and Sinai, by E. R. Vol. II. Outlying Countries.

"Of these two volumes, he hoped to be able to

finish at least the first. But God has decided otherwise. This first volume, of which the plan is distinctly laid out, he divided into three parts: 1. Physical Geography. 2. Historical Geography. 3. Topographical Geography.

"It pains me to say, that only the first part, the *Physical Geography*, is written; and even this not completely, for the last two chapters on Vegetable and on Animal Life, are still missing. They could, however, be easily supplied from the older manuscript, as there is no reason to believe that this portion of the work would have been materially altered by him. The seven hundred and fifty pages of this manuscript were written in exactly two years; or rather in the winter and spring months of two years; for during the months of July, August, and September he hardly ever wrote. They were commenced on the 3d of June, 1859, while the last page was written on the 3d of June, 1861. On the 18th of June his eye was operated upon, and he never was able to resume his studies."

Not for his own fame, which is safe, but for ourselves, and the whole living generation of Christian scholars, and for other generations yet unborn, do we lament the calamity of this unfinished work. There lives no man to finish it; and when one shall be born to do it, God only knows.

HIS LAST DAYS.

On the last days of our great scholar there fell the twilight of a fading vision. In both eyes a cataract had for some time been forming. The operation upon one eye, skillfully performed by Dr. Agnew on the 18th of June, 1861, failed of its desired effect. The age and other infirmities of the patient forbade success. In the latter part of May, 1862, Dr. Robinson set sail with his family for the old world, to avail himself of the professional advice of Dr. Graefe of Berlin, the most eminent oculist in Europe. He had the satisfaction, such as it was, of being assured by Dr. Graefe that his case had thus far been wisely managed, and that his American surgeon had done for him all that was possible under the circumstances. The seven weeks which were spent in the Infirmary at Berlin helped his general health ; but an operation upon the remaining eye was not deemed advisable, and he was compelled to leave, with nothing better to comfort him than the fact, that the cataract was making apparently no progress. Meanwhile, another disease, the nature of which was not then known, was undermining his constitution, and wasting his strength. And yet he had great enjoyment of life. In Switzerland he ascended the Rhigi. At Kösen, a watering-place near Halle, and wherever else his family went, he joined cheerfully in their recreations. In Halle he was very happy among the friends of his wife. In Berlin he had the society of Roediger, of Petermann, of Twesten, of Ranke, of Lepsius, of Wetstein, and of Kiepert. The attentions paid him by these distinguished scholars, who both admired and loved him, were not more flattering than friendly. The evenings they

spent together were as genial as any he had
ever known. He was enjoying, though he knew
it not, the mellow Indian summer of a life, which
was soon to close. He got back to New York
about the middle of November, and at once resumed his duties in the Seminary. On the 15th
of December the family physician was called in
to prescribe for new and more threatening symp-
toms, which had appeared. With the Christmas
holidays his labors ceased. And at half-past
nine o'clock on Tuesday evening, January 27th,
1863, he peacefully breathed his last. It is not
certain that he knew he was passing away.
Nor was it needful that he should. Behind him
lay a long life of faithful Christian service ; and
now, in dying, he had no new testimony to give.
Or if he knew that his time had come, he had
only to grasp silently the hand that was reached
out to him in the deepening shadow, and step
calmly through. And so he died. Had he lived
to see the 10th of April, he would have been
sixty-nine years old.

4*

With sorrow, which no words can measure, we now take our leave of this great, good man.

In summing up the achievements of his laborious career, it would be enough to recite the titles of his books ; but especially of three, which stand like monuments of granite piled up by his own hands. His record is : the best Greek Harmony as yet prepared ; the best Lexicon of the New Testament Greek in any language ; and a Journal of Travels in Palestine absolutely without a rival in the world. And yet the three are but one in impulse and intent. It was the supreme ambition of his life to explain and illustrate the Holy Bible. The one adjective in our language which he loved the most, was *Biblical.* It was the watchword of all his studies ; and now we carve it upon his tomb-stone. Of his special achievements in geography, it might suffice to say in general, what Ritter has so emphatically said, that Dr. Robinson's work on Palestine is the beginning of a new era in Biblical Geography. The readers of these volumes

do not need to be told, how many places spoken
of in the Bible he has identified, how many lying
legends he has routed. What if some call him
an iconoclast? Who wants to be cheated, even
into holy rapture over the Church of a sepulchre, which was somewhere else? At any cost,
let us have only the truth. It was he that did
more than any man had ever done before towards determining the true topography of Jerusalem, by identifying the fragment of an arch on
Mount Moriah with the bridge spoken of by
Josephus as leading from Moriah to Zion. A
desperate effort was made to tear this laurel
from his brow; but the laurel remained.* And
what he did for Jerusalem, he did also for the
whole of Palestine. It is hardly too much to

---

* Mr. Scoles, an English architect, had, some years before,
requested Mr. Catherwood to search for any remains which
there might be of the bridge of Josephus. In 1833 Mr.
Catherwood discovered the remnant of an arch, but so utterly
had the suggestion of Mr. Scoles faded from his memory,
that he thought of the arch only as belonging to some old
aqueduct or viaduct. Its *identification* was made by Dr.
Robinson in 1838.

say, that he found it afloat like an island in the
sea, almost like a cloud in the sky of fable, and
left it a part of Asia.

HIS CHARACTER.

Of his character, I might well hesitate to
speak ; for although some features of it were as
bold and rugged as the outline of Lebanon itself,
other features of it, little known to the world,
were as delicate and charming as the rose of
Sharon. His intellect was one of great native
solidity and vigor. For metaphysical subtleties
he had no relish whatever. What he sought for
was not truth in speculation, but truth in life ;
and, most of all, the truth of God, as revealed
for human guidance in duty. This, he thought,
might be surely known, and clearly stated. He
had great respect accordingly for the real *com-
munis sensus* of mankind ; and very little respect, some of us would say, not respect enough,
for the established terminology of the schools.
What he saw, he was determined to see clearly.

What he could not see clearly, he did not desire
to look at at all. If the word were not so commonly used in a bad sense exclusively, I should
say that he was naturally skeptical. But his
skepticism was of that sort which Bacon com-
mends in the Problems of Aristotle, which not
only " saveth philosophy from errors and false-
hoods," but serves also as a sucker or sponge
" to draw use of knowledge." Till he was quite
sure of a thing, he would not affirm it; and it
required more to assure him, than it does most
men. This trait was constantly appearing, even
in the most unreserved social intercourse; so
that his family used to call him " The Chancel-
lor," in allusion to some lines they had met with
in their reading :

> " Mr. Parker made the case darker,
>   Which was dark enough without;
> Mr. Leech made a speech,
>   And the Chancellor said: *I doubt.*"

And yet this habit of doubting, appears never to
have been let loose against the teachings of

Scripture. Persuaded, as he was so thoroughly, that man has need of a Divine revelation, and having satisfied himself that a Divine revelation has been made, and that the Bible is that revelation, he never dreamed of impugning its doctrines. His only question was : What are those doctrines? And when once established by a legitimate but rigid exegesis, he no longer treated them as aliens. What God had clearly spoken through Paul to the Romans, was as full of authority, and as final, to him, as what was spoken from Sinai to the Hebrews.

Being thus a man of clear and positive convictions, he was no less clear and positive in utterance. He had little facility, or power, in what is called *extempore* discourse. His thoughts came feebly to their birth upon his lips. But when he wrote, it was always with singular completeness, precision, and force. Sometimes there is great felicity of diction ; but commonly the beauty is of that severe sort, which gleams on the edge of the battle-axe. No man who pro-

voked him to controversy, cared ever to repeat
the experiment. He discovered to his cost, that
he might as well have put his fist between a trip-
hammer and its anvil. Whatever subject he
took in hand, he had a most searching and exhaustive way of treating it. No sheaf ever
came out from beneath his flail with much grain
left in it. As specimens of his controversial
skill and ability, we may instance his treatment
of Dr. Grant's attempted identification of the
Nestorians with the lost tribes of Israel; his
passage at arms with an English churchman
about the site of the Holy Sepulchre; his tri-
umphant vindication of his own claim to the
honor of discovery in the matter of the bridge
of Josephus; and the final disposition he made
of the vexed question with respect to marrying
the sister of a deceased wife. All these ques-
tions are now by most people thought to be settled. But with all this severity of method, and
all his diligence, he was not a dull, mechanical
worker. Stout as he was in make, he had great

fineness of fibre. In composition, he was always under the necessity of waiting upon his moods ; and wondered at the men who can write just when they will. Sometimes for days together he could make no headway in his higher tasks.

His scholarship was real, downright scholarship. It was also more various than was commonly supposed. In his earlier life, he played the flute, and was fond of poetry. With Shakespeare and Milton he was especially familiar. He was a careful reader of the best newspapers, religious and secular, and closely watched current events. It might almost be said, that what he failed to notice, was not worth noticing. He cherished no foolish conceit of independence upon the acquirements of those who had gone before him, in whatever department of study. He was guilty of no meanness in concealing the amount of his indebtedness to them. He used freely whatever lay open to be freely used. But he took the learning of others, whether dead or living, not for a Jacob's pillow to sleep on. but

for a Jacob's ladder to climb by. He began by
translating the works of others; he ended by
producing better works of his own. He exem-
plifies the great difference there is between
riding upon other men's backs, and standing
upon other men's shoulders. Unquestionably,
he had his full share of ambition as a scholar. His reputation, hard earned and slow
in coming, was precious to him; and he was
careful never to compromise it himself, nor per-
mit to be compromised by others. It is very
plain to me, from an inspection of his works,
that he expected them to live; and he accordingly weighed well his words. One seldom finds
in the writings of any man so many tokens of a
proper self-consciousness and self-respect. He
was not unaware of the important services he
was rendering, and had no lower aim, as surely
he could have had no higher, than to make those
services as effective for good as possible. A
touching example of this appears in his valedic-
tory to the patrons of the *Biblical Repository* in

1834, in which he says : "Under these circumstances, and bowed down with broken health, he
feels it to be a duty which he owes to himself, to
his family, and perhaps to the churches, to with-
draw from the station which he has hitherto
occupied as the conductor of a public Journal."
Of an overweening estimate of himself and his
services, I find nowhere any trace. Nor do I
know of any thing in his treatment of other
writers entering his special domain, to warrant
the charge against him of being " at once janitor
and judge, Cerberus and Rhadamanthus over all
travellers and books having relation to the Holy
Land."   A critical notice of the volumes of Mr.
Stephens, which he inserted in the *Commercial
Advertiser*, and which some pronounced severe,
Mr. Stephens himself was so well pleased with,
as to regret that it had not appeared in the
North American Review.   Certainly, no modest
scholar ever asked his assistance in any enterprise, without abundant occasion for gratitude ;
and no scholar ever added any thing to the

stock of human knowledge, without his applause.

He was likewise an able teacher; curt, blunt, and peremptory in manner, it is true; but always thoroughly master of his subject, and always best liked by the best scholars. He required no genius in his pupils, knowing well how rare that is; but he did require a proper deference to his opinions, and, above all, fidelity and diligence in study; and no man ever gave proof in his class-room of having slighted a lesson, without smarting for it. And yet his severity was never relentless. A student, whose remissness had greatly plagued him, and who had consequently suffered what he thought rather rough treatment at his hands, was one day overheard praying, that God would "bless Dr. Robinson, and teach him better manners." This prayer was reported to Dr. Robinson, and the result was, that the student, whether he deserved the relief or not, had less to complain of afterwards. Some years later, when that student happened to be in distress, Dr. Robinson took the lead in getting up a subscription in his behalf. Usually, the number of those in each successive class, who came into close personal relations with him, was small ; but the few who did know him socially, " knew him, but to love him," as now they " name him, but to praise." As an interpreter of Scripture, he may have leaned rather strongly towards a certain baldness of exegesis, as though he were in quest of the *minimum* of meaning ; but what he did find in a passage, you might be pretty sure was really there. His own favorite commentators were De Wette and Meyer ; not from sympathy with their doctrinal prepossessions, but because of their rigid adherence to what he considered the best method of interpretation. Meyer's Commentary on the New Testament, was one of the few books kept within easy reach upon the desk at which he studied. Hackett's *Acts*, it may be added, was another.

It is with the Union Theological Seminary,

that his fame as a scholar and teacher, will, in the time to come, be most intimately associated. Connected with it almost from its earliest beginning, devotion to its interests was one of the strongest passions of his life. Its metropolitan location commended itself to his judgment as affording some of the facilities for professional study most needed by candidates for the Christian ministry; while the perils involved, are only such as may serve to test and settle the character of the student. However long the institution may stand, and whatever may be its future enlargement, the first twenty-five years of its history will forever shine with the light of his labors and his renown. Till he returned from his first visit to Palestine he drew no pay from its treasury. To its alcoves he made large and valuable contributions from the shelves of his own library. On many of its alumni, who are now preaching the word of life, he set the stamp of a superior scholarship. Within the shadow of its walls he lighted for years his morning lamp ; performed a good part of the best work of his life ; and died at last with a reputation encircling the globe.

As a man he was little known. A natural reserve veiled his innermost character from the knowledge of the world. He might seem to be lethargic and unimpressible ; but in reality nothing which transpired in his presence escaped his notice. When he appeared to be seeing and hearing nothing, he was seeing and hearing all. Many people, no doubt, thought him to be hard and cold. He was any thing but hard and cold. The *"Homo sum"* of Terence, was never better exemplified than in him. The strong nervous element in his constitution, which exposed him to fits of melancholy, made him keenly alive to all human interests. He was also largely possessed of genuine humor, which seldom missed its opportunity. In the midst of grave discussions going on in his presence, I have heard from him, in an undertone, a by-play of pleasantry, which, if overheard, would have convulsed the audience with laughter. In any sorrow, which called for sympathy, his words were few, but his whole manner was so thoroughly tender and genial as never to be forgotten. In his own home, especially as he advanced in years and in reputation, his temper was delightful. No man was ever more fond of his wife ; or more considerate of the happiness of his children. In the common intercourse of life, no man was ever truer to his friends. As a citizen, no man was ever more intensely loyal to his country's flag ; or more ardent in praying for the time to come when that flag shall wave over only the free. Of his domestic life I have heard incidents, of which I forbear to speak. Of what occurred outside of the family circle, much might be reported which would set his character in a new light. Let one or two instances suffice. In former years, he used to write not a little for the newspapers. The money paid him for these articles commonly went into the pockets of indigent young men preparing for the Gospel ministry.

Only a few weeks before he died, happening to hear of a young man, once, though for a short time only, connected with the Seminary, as having come to the city for medical advice not likely to keep him from the grave, Dr. Robinson sent him a handsome sum of money through the hands of a friend, strictly charging that friend not to let the young man know who sent him the money. As the benefactor and the beneficiary are now both dead, I feel myself at liberty to divulge the secret. Many such good deeds went before him to his final account. If he had the head of a Jupiter, he had the heart of a child. Nor in these sad and shameful days of treason in arms behind its ramparts, and of a still baser treason *before* those ramparts, may we forget to commemorate, with thanksgiving and with pride, the burning patriotism of our departed friend. It was in him, and about him, like a flame of fire. Like all true scholars, like all good men, he loved his country as he loved the grave and the memory of his mother.

In his religious, as in his social character, Dr. Robinson was not at all demonstrative. It would be absurd to say, that his religion was not that of feeling; for religion is essentially a thing of feeling. But with him there was no forwardness in the expression of religious feeling. His life was a hidden one, and the deeper for being hidden. His peace with God appears to have been early made. I have not been able to learn at what time he joined himself to the visible communion of the Church. I only know, that in the earliest of his manuscripts which I have seen (and I have had before me sermons written when he was twenty-eight years of age), there are the clearest tokens of a well-advised and most settled faith in the person and work of the great Redeemer. The Gospel as a supernatural economy of healing and of help, is, in these sermons, surveyed with great distinctness of vision, and laid hold upon with great vigor and steadiness of grasp. He knew no other Christianity than that of the canonical Scrip-

5

tures, authenticated by miracles and prophecy.
He knew no way of being saved but by the grace
of God, abounding above his sin. And he knew
no warrant for his Christian hopes, but what
was furnished by his own patient continuance in
well-doing. He was never a parish clergyman ;
but during his residence at Andover he was li-
censed to preach by the Hartford Association in
Connecticut ; wrote in all nine sermons, leaving
also the fragment of a tenth, which are still preserved ; received Presbyterian ordination at the
hands of the Third Presbytery in this city, in
compliance with the requirements of the Constitution of the Seminary, when he became one of
its Professors ; and often preached in the earlier
part of his professional life, for the last time, I
believe, in one of the Dutch churches of this city
in 1846, although he has left no sermon written
later than 1826. Each of these sermons, is, in its
plan, exhaustive of the topic discussed, and all are
marked by great breadth and maturity of sentiment. His trial sermon, which he rarely

preached afterwards, was an elaborate discussion of the " Divine origin and authority of the Scriptures." His earliest popular discourse was on the " Danger of neglecting the Great Salvation." Other subjects were : " The Christian Race ; " " The Loss of the Soul ; " " Obedience, the Test of Christian Character ; " " Washing the Disciples' feet." The ninth, and last sermon completed by him, on " Preparation for Death," from the text, " I am now ready to be offered," I have read with peculiar interest. Had it been written thirty-six years later than it was, it could hardly have been any riper in Christian wisdom than it is. For myself, I am thankful to have had this opportunity for communion with so manly a piety. What he most valued in every Christian, was evidently that which he best exemplified in his own life : an abiding, hearty, practical interest in the earthly kingdom of his Lord and Master. For this he studied ; and for this he taught. His pupils have gone to the very ends of the earth. And no voice was

louder, or more urgent, than his in sending them.
The globe is dotted over with missionary posts,
at which the intelligence of his death will be
received with profoundest grief. The eternal
shore is now trodden by the feet of many pagan
converts, whose spiritual fathers were his children.

Alas, my father, thou art gone, to return no
more! That massive form will be seen no more
upon our surging streets. That deep voice will
be heard no more in the halls of Christian science. That sober, sturdy intellect will invite no
more the audience of learned men. That loyal
heart will beat no more in answer to the call of
country, or of home. The great scholar, one of
the greatest on our continent as yet, has done
his work, and folded his hands, and the account
is closed. "His body is buried in peace, but his
name liveth evermore."

AMERICA AND THE HOLY LAND

An Arno Press Collection

Adler, Cyrus and Aaron M. Margalith. **With Firmness in the Right:** American Diplomatic Action Affecting Jews, 1840-1945. 1946

Babcock, Maltbie Davenport. **Letters From Egypt and Palestine.** 1902

Badt-Strauss, Bertha. **White Fire:** The Life and Works of Jessie Sampter. 1956

Barclay, J[ames] T[urner]. **The City of the Great King.** 1858

Baron, Salo W. and Jeanette M. Baron. **Palestinian Messengers in America,** 1849-79. 1943

Bartlett, S[amuel] C[olcord]. **From Egypt to Palestine.** 1879

Bliss, Frederick Jones. **The Development of Palestine Exploration.** 1907

Bond, Alvan. **Memoir of the Rev. Pliny Fisk, A. M.:** Late Missionary to Palestine. 1828

Browne, J[ohn] Ross. **Yusef:** Or the Journey of the Frangi. 1853

Burnet, D[avid] S[taats], compiler. **The Jerusalem Mission:** Under the Direction of the American Christian Missionary Society. 1853

Call to America to Build Zion. 1977

Christian Protagonists for Jewish Restoration. 1977

Cox, Samuel S. **Orient Sunbeams:** Or, From the Porte to the Pyramids, By Way of Palestine. 1882

Cresson, Warder. **The Key of David.** 1852

Crossman, Richard. **Palestine Mission: A Personal Record.** 1947

Davis, Moshe, editor. **Israel:** Its Role in Civilization. 1956

De Hass, Frank S. **Buried Cities Recovered:** Or, Explorations in Bible Lands. 1883

[Even, Charles]. **The Lost Tribes of Israel:** Or, The First of the Red Men. 1861

Field, Frank McCoy. **Where Jesus Walked:** Through the Holy Land with the Master. 1951

Fink, Reuben, editor. **America and Palestine:** The Attitude of Official America and of the American People. 1944

Fosdick, Harry Emerson. **A Pilgrimage to Palestine.** 1927

Fulton, John. **The Beautiful Land:** Palestine, Historical, Geographical and Pictorial. 1891

Gilmore, Albert Field. **East and West of Jordan.** 1929

Gordon, Benjamin L[ee]. **New Judea:** Jewish Life in Modern Palestine and Egypt. 1919

Holmes, John Haynes. **Palestine To-Day and To-Morrow:** A Gentile's Survey of Zionism. 1929

Holy Land Missions and Missionaries. 1977

[Hoofien, Sigfried]. **Report of Mr. S. Hoofien to the Joint Distribution Committee of the American Funds for Jewish War Sufferers.** 1918

Intercollegiate Zionist Association of America. **Kadimah.** 1918

Isaacs, Samuel Hillel. **The True Boundaries of the Holy Land.** 1917

Israel, J[ohn] and H[enry] Lundt. **Journal of a Cruize in the U. S. Ship Delaware 74 in the Mediterranean in the Years 1833 & 34.** 1835

Johnson, Sarah Barclay. **Hadji in Syria:** Or, Three Years in Jerusalem. 1858

Kallen, Horace M[eyer]. **Frontiers of Hope.** 1929

Krimsky, Jos[eph]. **Pilgrimage & Service.** 1918-1919

Kyle, Melvin Grove. **Excavating Kirjath-Sepher's Ten Cities.** 1934

Kyle, Melvin Grove. **Explorations at Sodom:** The Story of Ancient Sodom in the Light of Modern Research. 1928

Lipsky, Louis. **Thirty Years of American Zionism.** 1927

Lynch, W[illiam] F[rancis]. **Narrative of the United States' Expedition to the River Jordan and the Dead Sea.** 1849

Macalister, R[obert] A[lexander] S[tewart]. **A Century of Excavation in Palestine.** [1925]

McCrackan, W[illiam] D[enison]. **The New Palestine.** 1922

Merrill, Selah. **Ancient Jerusalem.** 1908

Meyer, Isidore S., editor. **Early History of Zionism in America.** 1958

Miller, Ellen Clare. **Eastern Sketches:** Notes of Scenery, Schools, and Tent Life in Syria and Palestine. 1871

[Minor, Clorinda]. **Meshullam!** Or, Tidings From Jerusalem. 1851

Morris, Robert. **Freemasonry in the Holy Land.** 1872

Morton, Daniel O[liver]. **Memoir of Rev. Levi Parsons, Late Missionary to Palestine.** 1824

Odenheimer, W[illiam] H. **Jerusalem and its Vicinity.** 1855

Olin, Stephen. **Travels in Egypt, Arabia Petraea, and the Holy Land.** 1843. Two Vols. in One

Palmer, E[dward] H[enry]. **The Desert of the Exodus.** 1871. Two Vols. in One

Paton, Lewis Bayles. **Jerusalem in Bible Times.** 1908

Pioneer Settlement in the Twenties. 1977

Prime, William C[ooper]. **Tent Life in the Holy Land.** 1857

Rifkind, Simon H., et al. **The Basic Equities of the Palestine Problem.** 1947

Rix, Herbert. **Tent and Testament:** A Camping Tour in Palestine with Some Notes on Scriptural Sites. 1907

Robinson, Edward. **Biblical Researches in Palestine, Mount Sinai and Arabia Petraea.** 1841. Three Volumes

Robinson, Edward. **Later Biblical Researches in Palestine and in Adjacent Regions.** 1856

Schaff, Philip. **Through Bible Lands:** Notes on Travel in Egypt, the Desert, and Palestine. [1878]

Smith, Ethan. **View of the Hebrews.** 1823

Smith, George A[lbert], et al. **Correspondence of Palestine Tourists.** 1875

Smith, Henry B[oynton] and Roswell D. Hitchcock. **The Life, Writings and Character of Edward Robinson.** 1863

Sneersohn, H[aym] Z[vee]. **Palestine and Roumania.** 1872

Szold, Henrietta. **Recent Jewish Progress in Palestine.** 1915

Talmage, T[homas] de Witt. **Talmage on Palestine:** A Series of Sermons. 1890

Taylor, Bayard. **The Lands of the Saracen:** Or, Pictures of Palestine, Asia Minor, Sicily, and Spain. 1855

The American Republic and Ancient Israel. 1977

Thompson, George, et al. **A View of the Holy Land.** 1850

Van Dyke, Henry. **Out-of-Doors in the Holy Land:** Impressions of Travel in Body and Spirit. 1908

Vester, Bertha [Hedges] Spafford. **Our Jerusalem:** An American Family in the Holy City, 1881-1949.   1950

Wallace, Edwin Sherman. **Jerusalem the Holy.**   1898

[Ware, William]. **Julian:** Or Scenes in Judea.   1841. Two Vols. in One

Worsley, Israel. **A View of the American Indians:** Showing Them to Be the Descendants of the Ten Tribes of Israel.   1828

Yehoash [Bloomgarden, Solomon]. **The Feet of the Messenger.**   1923

LIBRARY OF DAVIDSON COLLEGE

Books on regular loan may be checked out for **two weeks.** Books must be presented at the Circulation Desk in order to be renewed.

A fine is charged after date due.

Special books are subject to special regulations at the discretion of library staff.